The Air We Breathe
Alys Hall

Copyright © 2024 Barnard Publishing Ltd

All rights reserved

Disclaimer; This is a work of fiction. Unless otherwise indicated, all the names, characters, businesses, places, events, and incidents in this book are either the product of the author's imagination or used in a fictitious manner. Any resemblance to actual persons, living or dead, or actual events is purely coincidental.

The Air We Breathe © Alys Hall

Cover design by Mari Hall

ISBN 978-1-7394744-0-9

Barnard Publishing Ltd
Wales

barnard.publishing@gmail.com

www.barnardpublishing.co.uk

one breath	7
i waited	9
pili pala (noun): welsh for 'butterfly'.	10
painted lady	11
the forest's voice	12
coastline	13
llwybrau	14
the place	15
POV: the sea	16
snails	17
pysgota	18
ar goll! missing!	19
the squirrel	20
tir	21
the graveyard	22
why does the sky cry?	23

overheating	24
llwynog r. williams parry	25
roadsides	26
yesterday	27
par tic les	28
routines on planet earth	29
guilt	30
ethical quandary	31
what it might mean to love the earth	32
access to water	34
what can we do?	35
your little grain of sand	36
the air we breathe	37
Context	38

Dedication:
For Isabelle Simón
For Friends of the Earth

one breath

the sky has shattered to pieces
the sea has swallowed my heart
the wind has heard my sorrow
and the rain has torn me apart

the air we breathe is suffocating
the earth is mourning a death
the sparrow is eating its young
all there is left is one ounce
of a breath

yet with one breath will come two
the grass will grow all the same
our paths are not set in stone
they might yet remember our names

pilipala
pilipala pili
pala butterfly butter
fly butterfly butter   pilipala   manteu
mariposa mariposa fritillary fritillary butterfly
vanessa cardui vanessa cardui painted
lady where did all the butterflies go
the small skipper peacock butterfly
celastrina celastrina argiolus
las mariposas ¿dónde están las
mariposas? ble mae'r pilipala
i'a y pilipala pilipala glöyn byw
iârfach yr Haf butterfly papillon
farfalla motyl Schmetterling vlin
der leptir pili sommerfugl pili
pala pala ble mae' on
pili pala on
pala

i waited

i waited for the butterflies
and i waited for the stream
it was on the shoreline i waited
for a love to be returned
and on farmland i waited
for birdsong to begin at dawn

i waited motionless
for life to begin
when it had begun
i waited for my song to change
when it was… always is
perfectly imperfect

i waited in vain
for something already there
that, here, remains

pili pala (noun): welsh for 'butterfly'.

though the butterfly can't hear
in the strict sense
the hustle and bustle
outside open windows
they sense no less

no less do they sense
hurried whispers between lovers
a frog's ribbit in the grass
a wine glass clink

da-awel nôs
sanctaidd yw´r nôs…
like this i sang
hoping the sounds might reach
the tip of each antennae

the butterfly can hear
sound waves vibrating
frequencies across membranes
so, in truth, sensing sound

like this the pili pala hears
without the need for ears

painted lady

i don't know much about you
no – i don't claim to know
anything at all

you flew near a tricoloured buddleia
awash with vibrance and i –
stunned – happened to see you
fluttering flapping flying
no fear of falling

you flew near a different precipice
near latent knowledge
of a language lying hidden
floating between worlds

there you flew among
fuschias   geraniums   roses
painting the sky   speckling it

the forest's voice

not far from here there is a world in a world
home to birds, badgers, fish and flowers
where it is wealth itself to know each nook,
tree and trough.

it's where you ask the tree permission
to trace the trunk with fingertips
you ask to feel the fuzziness of veined leaves
hear the sounds of the stream...
the universe in the stones...
the bird's poem...
silence.

now close the lids of your tired eyes
and next you will listen to the ...

coastline

the redshank wades the shoreline
coral beak collects
as footprints trail behind

they leave webs in the sand
where the sea holds the land

the golden shore opens a trove of
wet shells glistening

they stretch across miles of coastline
where they arrive and retreat
arrive and retreat

the seagulls swoop
broaden their wings wide
held by the air they stagger
before skydiving
headlong down

they disturb the guillemots who sit
pensive   ushered by waves
goaded by winds
they chatter with tales
about the sea and its sky

llwybrau

we trudge along footpaths
llwybr clawdd offa … arfordir môn
collecting memories by the shore

a swallow dips   then soars
landing on skeletal trees like antlers
a bronchial web in our lungs

we pass new cottages
devoid of all but the crow's tale
atop cold chimneys
as we collect our pennies
dywedwn nid yw gymru ar werth
we say our country is not for sale
these words that fall unnoticed

the sky darkens   dims its hue
reveals a round head and silent wings
an owl in flight. we pause
stunned by its grace
we witness these moments here
feel the universe folded in them

our pockets are near empty
our hearts? hopeful
(perhaps foolishly)
they are bravely full

the place

i'll take you to the place
where daisies open at night
and close by day
foreshadowing an eclipse
foregoing photosynthesis

moonlight preserves the petal's sanity
seeds emerge from the bark
emerge from furred leaves

green leaves wither in fragments
fall apart for dust
regenerating in spring
for the purposes of blooming
in a spring held here

let me take you to the place
where we can see and feel
the earth in a different way

to the place where the garden path
is not linear

POV: the sea

endless depth wave after wave
I carry the world's ships
cause some to capsize

I meet the land lap the shore
move sands crash against rocks
drown paths and trails

I obey the moon's laws
and move the tides
I am home to whales
krill coral reefs plankton
I am home to the fish
all manner of algae

but I am now under threat

my reefs whiten   I am now
home to oil-spills
blackened by pollution
I hold islands of plastic
that feed my fish
nets strangle the turtles
debris floats washes waves
bottles from previous decades

though some who carry kindness
disperse it – they collect the crates
accumulated on the shore
cut nets   save my inhabitants
clear the debris   nurture
me – this body of water –
so that I may for years
centuries more
continue to flow   to house
and to hold

snails

    we chart the traces of their shells
                            that swirl in shining spirals
                                                resplendent
                          scattered on sand
        hollow and waterlogged
with sea salt
                snails are slow
                          and have long memories
                                              traces in their
trails
                        trapped in footprints
          speckles worn over time
                              the snails remember

pysgota
      |
         fishing
           |

the trawler drags a net along the seabed
mechanised modernity
hauling fish in droves
they rig out at sea

white skies   clouded
hazed sun   lauded

harvesting sharks
finning them for soup
they suffocate finless
hammerheads blacktips whitetips

discarding waste
meeting critical quotas
in monitored logbooks

human bodies are left
beached on the coast
in a world without fish

ar goll! missing!

mae'r ci defaid ar goll
the sheepdog is missing
dywedodd yr arwydd

treading milltiroedd
of land   sheer stretches
the wind goads him on relentless

at home the wind clinks the chimes
outside yr hen ffarm
metal catches metal by chance
callers chatter about the sheepdog
as he follows his inner compass home

the seagulls follow the tractor
dipping for leatherjackets
as the plough lifts the earth
each blade slices the surface
clattering against rocks in lines
to turn green grass brown
cutting   loosening fresh soil
the farmer ploughs   absent

mae'r ci defaid ar goll!
the sheepdog is missing!
cold he quivers the compass needle
until he sources a trail
to tread along and follow   adre

the squirrel

the lichen spreads moss carpets
twigs are strewn scattered
across miles of forest floor
tucked in   away from sight
the acorns hide

I climb great heights
enormous pillars with no
branches in sight
my red coat snags
the bark and my tail bobs
behind   follows

below flashers poised
they watch stunned –
stood on the footpath
my existence is extraordinary.
I appear red coat gleaming -
they click flash murmur…
I scurry away suspicious
of these strange animals.

tir

Troesom ein tir yn simneiau tân   *We turned our land into chimneys of fire*
a phlannu coed a pheilonau cadarn   *and planted robust trees and pylons*
lle nad oedd llyn.   *where there was no lake.*
    'Etifeddiaeth' by Gerallt Lloyd Owen, 'Cerddi'r Cywilydd' (1972)

chimneys of fire –
the legacy of this land
that will outlast our choirs

dried-up lakes
burnt yellow fields
cracks where earth breaks

chopped up trees
in our carelessness
businessmen to please

our planet three degrees
we ignore Greta's pleas
oil companies to appease

but it is the seeing
that frees.

our chimneys of fire –
make our world drier.
what use are my rhymes
in the face of these crimes?

the graveyard

imagine fields blackened
burnt to ash
trunks hollowed
all set aflame

envision angry flames
leaving black trees like veins
no stones to mark their names
a graveyard with nameless graves

look at these black skeletons
who remain standing
memories of who they once were

never put to rest   look
at the havoc we have wrought
on the blanket of this sweet earth

why does the sky cry?

a little face tilts up to see
a sticky sky
once suffocatingly dry

eyes like orbs stop to stare
as cars whizz by
her small hands point
at the droplets dripping
from the sky to slam the earth
filling the desperate cracks

in a small voice she asks
(having never seen rain)
mama, why does
the sky
cry?

overheating

remember the sight of ice
it will melt soon enough
this is humanity's price -
this truth we find too tough

it will melt soon enough
and the sea will rise
this truth we find too tough
it will happen before our eyes

and the sea will rise
everything will be drowned
it will happen before our eyes
and we will seek higher ground

everything will be drowned
this is humanity's price -
and we will seek higher ground
remember the sight of ice

llwynog r. williams parry

r. williams parry's fox

mae'r beic
the bike

yn osgoi
Swerves

côt goch ar lawr   yn y ffordd
red fur lies   in the road

mwdlyd   mae'r pryfaid yn casglu
muddied   the flies gather

arogl afiach
unbearable stench

y llygaid yn ddau dwll   clustiau difywyd
holes for eyes   lifeless ears

be roedd unwaith yn rhywun
what was once someone

wedi'i syfrdanu cyn marwolaeth
stunned at the moment of death

rwan yn gwrthrych   heb fynegiad
now something   expressionless

wedi'i llyncu gan y concrit
swallowed by concrete   yn arnofio yn y gofod
                                      floating in space

tragwyddol
eternal

roadsides

there i saw balled up
on the hard shoulder
covered in spines
diminished

vehicles whizzed by
shocked then scattered
to the side
rolled into a ball
exposed

partner and baby await
nesting together tightly
in the hedge
expectant

when will we realise
they share
this air
we breathe?

yesterday

those who shoulder
the globe aflame
are dying
muted on screen
and stage   lips moving
voices travelling
to closed ears
no water to drink
a stream ran dry
for greed yesterday
indigenous land was stolen
yesterday
they were told to adapt
yesterday
and today
they can hear
but refuse to listen.

                                                                                              par tic les

                                    par tic les found in p   lacentas
                                                                    fet   al mem bra ne
                                        un   born
                                                                 breath e & con   sume
b   irth plas   tic
                                          prod p   article s
                                                             babies   pre   polluted
p arents' pro bab le con   cern
                                                       fo   reign bo   dies in stre ams
                                     bl oo d   screams
                                                                                       in organic
                                                                                         to   x   ic
                                          un   developed

routines on planet earth

i shelled out my insides
to make room for oil

i filled my cup with oil
poured it into my palm
drank it with a side of coal

i gulped the oil and it dripped
in dollops along my lips

i bathed in oil
showered in it each day
and used it as a condiment

spread it on my toast
and toasted with it in glasses

i came to cry oil
from my lids
it ran in streams
and i wore it   proud

don't look up
don't look ahead
look at my dress
how many miles she travelled
look at how much oil she holds

and look at my shoes
look how they glisten with oil
look at how they shine

guilt

i can't help but wonder
about the care i feel
the tears i have shed
on the earth's blanket
as their eyes bone dry
shine with greed

it is i who feels guilt
for all i have and haven't done
for unrecycled bottles
for meat i consumed last month

ethical quandary

if i bit into this shirt
tasted the sweat in the cotton
i might see that what i wear
make my words rotten

how can i stand here
children's blood in the stitches -
oil dripping on the inside
for someone else's riches?

what it might mean to love the earth

what if on this earth
we watch where the
hermit crab goes?

let's watch how they
burrow under sands
hidden beneath our bare feet

let's watch where
they go when they
move to a more
spacious shell

tell me: what causes the crab
to change shells?
what causes the caterpillar
to create a chrysalis?

when reasoning is futile
when answers evade us
let's for a moment
just watch
as they move on
let's watch them
enjoying this earth
we share

gratitude

- the first drops of rain
- the sound of sea waves
- wild, overgrown gardens
- the grass tickling your feet
- a seedling breaking the surface of the soil
- a cat purring
- birds singing at dawn
- moments of presence

access to water

under the light of a half-moon
the lake swallows stillness
leaves ripple the surface
solitary circles swallow sound

the air sticks to your skin
delirious   you don't move
yet sweat all the same
dŵr… dŵr… dŵr…
water! water! water!
only for perspiration
to coat your skin

hot air clogs your lungs
you're drowning
gasping for air to breathe
raking for it empty-handed
until you collapse   defeated

at forty degrees the hypothalamus
starts to suffer
at forty degrees our brain
suffocates

and so you ask the lake
gently to hold you
envelop the heaviness

as you were born in the north
here in this watered
air-conditioned privilege

what can we do?

what love can spring in times of trouble
when rivers are dry and our future in rubble?
what can one do in the midst of this ache
an aching for a world made just
for all… not just for some?

what difference can be made
if one word could be changed
from what one can do
to what we can do

in this way love springs
and in this way rivers run
it's in the hope that we find
and in the aches undone

so hold your fear like a lamb
then let it go and see:
what one cannot do alone
can be done when you say "we"

your little grain of sand

from the Spanish phrase 'aportar tu granito de arena.' In English, it is to do your part for the planet, literally 'to contribute your little grain of sand'.

we each hold a grain of sand
in the crook of our hand
how we contribute our grain
won't all be the same

some will plant seeds
others tend to the trees
some keep their grain for greed
no thought for the earth's needs

each of us will leave footprints
in the sands of time
tell me: will you tread the earth kindly
or mark the ground with force?
tell me: will your little grain
give us the hope we must gain?

the air we breathe

there is a memory i keep
of air clean as freshwater
where your palms are leaves
your toes are the roots

there is a calm, they say,
before the storm -
or is it after?

will you remember
the unhazed sun?
a gulp of air unchoked
from a memory we hold
in the north

there is a memory i keep
of air clean as freshwater
tucked away for now
always hoped

it is this air we share
that invisible bond
from which we depend
inhale. exhale.
this is your life.

context

14 - "Nid yw cymru ar werth´´: ´Wales is not for sale´. This slogan appears in many Welsh communities affected by the issue of second homes. Organisations such as Cymdeithas yr Iaith (the Society for the Welsh Language) are campaigning for restrictions to be put in place on the sale of second homes and the high number of holiday homes appearing in these communities. In these areas, Welsh is widely spoken and the language is put under threat as local people who would otherwise buy or rent a home in their own communities are unable to do so due to prices skyrocketing in these areas. ´Nid yw Cymru ar Werth´ protests have called for the government to respect these communities' wishes and aid the housing crisis.

25 - R Williams Parry's fox: The poem Y Llwynog (The Fox) by R. Williams Parry is a classic in Welsh literature. It is widely taught in Welsh schools and it describes the poet's unexpected encounter with a fox on the hill. The poem urges the reader to marvel at these unexpected occurrences and the beauty of nature. Yet, in the world that we inhabit today, R. Williams Parry's fox would face the challenges of modern industrialisation…

Alys Hall is a writer and poet from North Wales. Her writing seeks to give space to environmental concerns, the LGBTQ+ community and Welsh myth. She published Into the Light (2022) with Barnard Publishing, as well as Sonder: An Anthology alongside her MA Creative Writing peers at Bangor University. You can find her Instagram @alys.catrin.

Becca Barnard was born in Bedford and moved to Wales in 2015. Reading has always been a huge part of her life, from her dad reading The Hobbit to her and her sister before bed, to writing her own fiction (and fanfiction) on Wattpad. She was the first student to achieve a degree in Publishing and Book Culture at Bangor University, and started Barnard Publishing Ltd in response to a lack of publishers in the North, especially in Wales. Also, she hopes one day to join forces with her dad at Barnard Engineering to build Barnard Corp., and one day rule the universe.

Barnard Publishing Ltd was established July 2022 and began trading that following November following the completion of Becca's Masters degree. Beneath the Poisoned Roots is her first publication, and Barnard Publishing has since taken it into its catalogue, hence this new edition.

www.ingramcontent.com/pod-product-compliance
Lightning Source LLC
Chambersburg PA
CBHW011557070526
44585CB00023B/2641